784.2
RAC

Rachmaninoff, Sergei, 1873-1943

Symphony No. 2 in E Minor, Op. 27

	DATE DUE		
MAY 06 2004			

Symphony No. 2
in E Minor, Op. 27
in Full Score

Serge Rachmaninoff

DOVER PUBLICATIONS, INC.
Mineola, New York

—

Bibliographical Note

This Dover edition, first published in 1999, is a republication of an authoritative early edition. Lists of contents and instrumentation are newly added.

International Standard Book Number: 0-486-40624-6

Manufactured in the United States of America
Dover Publications, Inc., 31 East 2nd Street, Mineola, N.Y. 11501

CONTENTS

Composed 1906–7.
Dedicated to Sergey Ivanovich Taneyev.

INSTRUMENTATION

3 Flutes [Flauti, Fl.]
  Fl. III doubles Piccolo

3 Oboes [Oboi, Ob.]

English Horn [Corno inglese, C. ingl.]

2 Clarinets in A, B♭ ("B") [Clarinetti, Clar.]

Bass Clarinet in A, B♭ ("B") [Clarinetto basso, Cl. basso]

2 Bassoons [Fagotti, Fag.]

4 Horns in E [Corni, Cor.]

3 Trumpets in A, B♭ ("B") [Trombe, Tr.]

3 Trombones [Trombone, Tromb.]

Tuba

Timpani [Timpani, Timp.]

Percussion
  Glockenspiel
  Snare Drum [Tamburo]
  Cymbals & Bass Drum [Piatti e Gr(an) Cassa]

Violins I, II [Violino, Viol.]

Violas [Viola]

Cellos [Violoncello]

Basses [Basso]

Symphony No. 2
in E Minor, Op. 27

I.

Poco più mosso. (♩ = 58)

Poco più mosso. (♩ = 58)

a tempo più mosso (♩=66)

14

a tempo più mosso (♩=66)

14

32 [I]

15 *poco a poco crescendo e agitato*

15 *poco a poco crescendo e agitato*

34   [I]

19 poco a poco calando e rit.

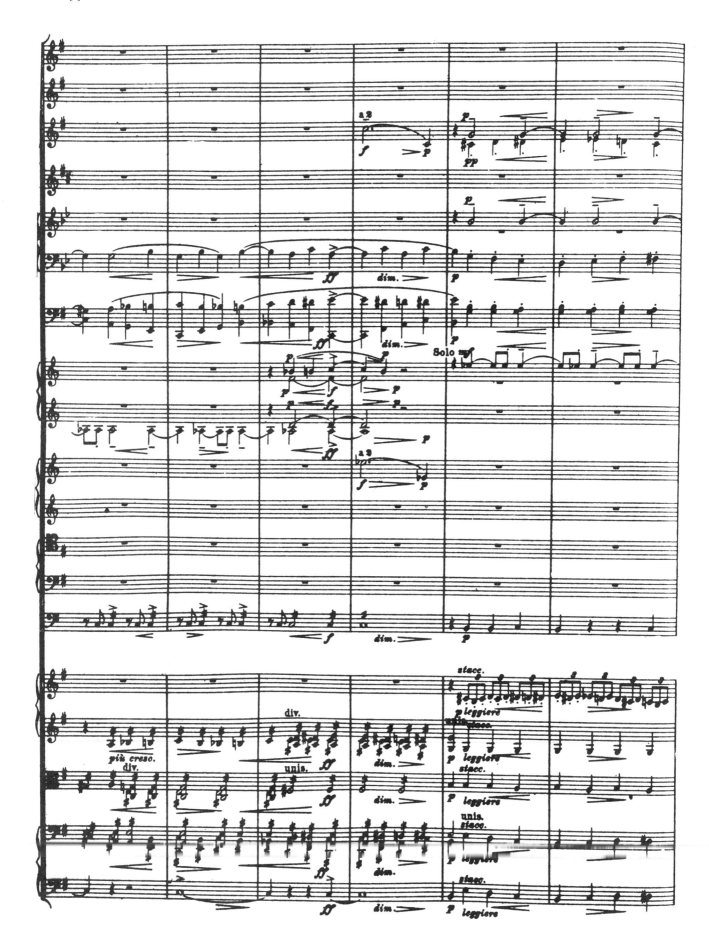

62   [I]

II.

72 [II]

Moderato.

Moderato.

Con moto.

Con moto.

90 [II]

Poco a poco accelerando al tempo I.

Tempo I.

Tempo I.

Moderato.

Moderato.

Con moto.

Con moto.

III.

Poco più mosso.

Poco più mosso.

IV.

Allegro vivace. ($\quad$ = 84-92)

Flauti I. II.

Flauto III
e poi Piccolo.

3 Oboi. I. II.

III.

2 Clarinetti in A.

Clarinetto basso in A.

2 Fagotti.

4 Corni in E. I. II.

III. IV.

3 Trombe in A. I. II.

III.

Trombone I. II.

Trombone III
e Tuba.

Timpani
in Gis. H. Dis.

Glockenspiel.

Piatti e Gran Cassa.

Violino I.

Violino II.

Viola.

Violoncello.

Basso.

Allegro vivace. ($\quad$ = 84-92)

150

156 [IV]

Con moto.

Con moto.

a tempo (♩=88=92)

196 [IV]

Più mosso.

Più mosso.

228 [IV]

END OF EDITION